Author of this book

Mr. B Senthil Kumar who is the author of this book belongs to Coimbatore. He is a graduate from Amrita Institute of Technology and Science, Coimbatore in electronics and communication engineering and MBA graduate from Bharathiar University. Completed his certificate course in Export Management.

He is having 12 of years of working experience in companies like ok ITC, Horlicks, and Himalaya as a Area Sales Manager.

He is running a YouTube channel "BLUE BULLET" for business entrepreneurs and job seekers for career development. He is a social activist. Wrote many articles, blogs in Politics, Cinema and Economy, Business in Newspaper and Social media like blog, Twitter and Face book.

With his 12 years of experience in sales and marketing in the FMCG industry as well as the Export industry, he comes up with the book for budding Exporters to successfully startup an Export Business in India with 100% practical exercises and explanations.

I0480537

B.SenthilkumarMBA

INTRODUCTION

Before we start any business we should know the basics of that business. We should collect the data and information about the business, and we should be familiar with the pros and cons of the business.

A Person should have a clear business plan to start and run the business. All these exercises will never be thought within a day and I came across many budding exporters who lost their money, time and peace because of the wrong guidance. Then only started framing this book for helping the Budding exporters to start their export business.

In this book, I am not explaining about the process of getting IE code, GST, PAN number. The book is going to explain the step by step procedures to start you and establish an export business in India. and the book is brief about what are all the exercises the budding exporters should do to be familiar with the export business.

I believe that this book will help the budding exporters who interested in the export business, the industry which brings foreign currency into the nation and helps to develop the domestic economy that can help the nation.

Why we have to start a business.

In today's world scenario and lifestyle, that leads to instability in everyone's financial position and the career. Though it's a government job or private job the situation is similar everywhere. In that situation, starting up an own business will give confidence to individuals financially as well as careers. In this globalized world, there are many opportunities are born day by day. our work is to identify those opportunities and utilize the same.

This world is looking for new and innovative entrepreneurs. Newcomers are looking for new opportunities. Entrepreneurs who realize those opportunities and needs are immediately more likely to succeed in the business world.

What is an export business?

Export trade is the trade of goods and services from one country to another.

Why should we do trade exports?

Every country in the world needs all kinds of goods. A few products are less likely to be produced in that country according to its requirements. For example, although gasoline is abundant in the Arab countries, the country is lagging in its food production. So that country depends on other countries for food products. Similarly, a few countries produce certain products that are more than their needs. Export and import trade is needed to balance this difference

Any nation needs to increase exports to boost its economic growth because export trade increases the country's foreign exchange.

So those involved in the export trade directly participate in the economic development of the nation. This book is teaches you only how to start an export business successfully in India.

Export Business

Export business is the export of services and products from India to other countries

Basic qualifications to do export business

There are no basic age, educational requirements for doing business in export.

But export trade means the sale of goods or services to a person or company in another Country.

So if you have the basic educational qualifications for communication, understanding the export business and conducting business effectively.

You need to know to understand that,all the communication are done in English. So understand the basic english or with the help of person who can be able to speak,write and work in English will help to run the business effectively.

Types of exporters

In India, exporters are classified into four types

1.Manufacturing exporters

2.Merchant export

3.Service exporters

4.Project exporters

now we will discuss the above exporters

Manufacturing exporters

Exporters who produce the goods on their own manufacturing unit or industry and supply the stock domestic need, as well as foreign trade, are called manufacturing exporter .

Pro's

The product price is in their control.

They can customize the product as per the importer's need.

They will get the subsidy and offers from government

institutions.

Con's

To Set up a manufacturing unit huge investment is needed.

There is a need for warehouses to store the raw material as well as a finished good.

Manufacturing exporter should maintain and manage various departments like production, Finance, human resources etc.

Merchant exporters

They are the intermediaries who get stocks from the manufacturer and export to foreign countries.

Pros

No need for heavy investment for setting up an industry as like manufacturing exporter.

Their marketplace's opportunities are bigger.

They can export multiple products.

Con

They can't customize the product as per the importer's need.

Service exporters

Software export BPO, medical transcription, International Courier agencies, International manpower Agencies are falling under the service exporter category.

Project exporters

Project exporters are the exporters who work for bigger projects like constructing a bridge Dam, big civil works, erection, planning, and designing.

Two types of business

Business to Business (B2B)

Business to Consumer (B2C)

Exercise

Write down any 50 business to business products

Write down any 50 business to consumer products

How to select products for export business?

The most important thing is to choose the right products for the export business. One of the main reasons why exporters fail in business not chooses the right products. So you have to be very careful in selecting products for export

Here are some ideas for selecting products for the newly exporting entrepreneurs

1. Too many exports, too much competition. So avoid competitive products.

2. Choose your favorite on select items

It is necessary to be content

3. Selected goods for export of time and time

We have to be willing to spend to read about

4. It is convenient to be near the place where we live (home/town/city/district).

5. PERISHABLE GOODS

The exclusion of goods is good. There will be at least 3 months of SHELF LIFE. Must be commodities.

6. Price fluctuations in the new export business

Avoid excessive items.

7. Budding exporters should avoid products which high technical specifications. Technical specifications are items that need much more Avoided.

8. Avoid the products which are banned, prohibited by FTP.

9. Try to select the products which are falls under mass consumption.

10. New exporters are beginning to learn about the export business with the idea of Rice, Cotton, Textile, Spices. But realize that millions of products are exported in the export business

Exercise

Write down 50 end product per the below category

Mass consumption product

Perishable goods

Ask for the trade policy categories, products are categorized into three different segments

Free trade products

Restricted product

Prohibited products

Exercise

Write down 50 product names for the above categories

The product which is highly exported from India

1 Spices

2 Agro products

3 textiles

4 leather product

5 Silk products

6 plastic

7 Handmade and Handloom products

8 cotton

9 tea and coffee

10 Gems and Jewels

11 Pharma products

12 sports types of equipment

13 Engineering goods

14 Chemicals

15 Nuts

HARMONIZED SYSTEM CODE (HS CODE)

The export business is sending the product from one country to another country. The product which is called in one name is different in another country so this difference should not affect the business. For that code for a particular product is design by the World Trade Organisation called as a harmonized system i.e HS CODE

HS code is having eight digits

First two-digit are called chapter
2nd two-digit are called group
Next two digits are called subgroup
Final 2 digits are indicating

Example

Rice (HS CODE) - 10 06 30 20

Wheat (HS CODE) - 10 01 99 10

Fish (HS CODE) - 16 04 11 00

Exercise

Write down the HS code for the product which you have written in the above exercises, using internet.

Here are some tips for naming an export company

1. Avoid naming the company with too many words.

   It is easy to name at least six characters.

2. The company name should be easily understood by people from other

   Countries.

3. It is good to have a name that makes them easy to pronounce

   An example is Apple, Amazon

4. It is easy to put the three letters in italics.

5. You can name the products you have selected for export.

   It's easy to get into the minds of traders

How to get the orders in export business?

Getting orders is the most important thing in any business. That is the basis of a business. In such a competitive world, it is difficult to get sales orders for their products

Some people enter the export business with no prior experience, some in the export business, some working in private export business.

Websites such as B2B portals, such as ALIBABA, TRADE INDIA, INDIA MART, etc., introduce new importers to new exporters.

Also Trade Shows, trade meetings Exporters can also get buyers for their products.

One of the most important tools for export trade with the world is the internet communication tools WEBSITES, B2B MARKETPLACES, email and more.

E-Commerce

What are the websites?

Websites is the address to the business we run. It is open 24 hours a day, 7 days a week. Our shop is open 365 days of the year. It helps you reach more customers with less investment.

This is where we advertise our products. Those who need the products we export can start their business here through Enquiry..

ONLINE BANKING can be done to get money from customers.

DOMAIN NAME (company's web address)

DOMAIN NAME is the name of our company on the website. It can usually be ended with .com, .in, net, .org

Get as much contact with the world countries as possible at our DOMAIN NAME .com EXTENSION

EXERCISES

export companies' websites navigate to their DOMAIN NAME, TEMPLATE and try to understand them.

Some suggestions

Don't design your websites with the free template available on the web.

Start a website with a small investment to pay the web site professionals

Doing so will be DYNAMIC WEBSITE and it will be helpful to be DYNAMIC WEBSITE when you need to make any changes.

Important information to be placed on websites

1. HOME

The year the company was founded, by whom

Business value, how many employees work, of the company

MISSION, VISION, PRODUCTS, CONTACT Etc

2. Products photos

Video or photo materials of the prepared method

SPECIFICATIONS INCLUDING DETAILS

3. Update photos and videos of products

Avoid uploading from web sites

4. CONTACT DETAILS

Address Telephone Mail ID Personal Information

SEAR CH ENGINE OPTIMIZATION (SEO)

Most people who use the Internet will be familiar with SEO called SEARCH ENGINE OPTIMIZATION. It is a technology that helps our website to be ranked at the top of the Google search engine in millions of websites.

Finding BUYERS is one of the most important things for newcomers to the export business. The Google web search engine makes it easy. For Example an Importer of rice in Arab country will search in google with a keyword like "Rice Exporter in India". Google will list down all the exporters from India who send Rice to Arab countries based on SEO Concept, the name of the exporter will be seen in the first page of google.

That's why any company tries to put their company's name on Google's search engine to be the number one on a business search engine.

Exporters who are new to the export business are committed to getting orders as much as possible through this SEO SEARCH ENGINE OPTIMIZATION to put their business company name on the Google search engine.

EXERCISE

Write KEYWORDS for products that you have selected for export at least 50 KEYWORDS.

Email Business (E-MAIL MARKETING)

Email is the most important place in the export business. Communication and trade-offs with importers and manufacturers from other countries should only take place via e-mail.

When an item is only required by email, they are stored as files when prices are disputed, quotations are sent and received, and finally cash transactions. They can also be helpful in case of later problems with cash or merchandise.

EXERCISES

Write down the letters on below topics:

Business proposal mail
Product inquiry reply mail
Product specification reply mail
Product specification confirmation mail
Product pricing request mail
Product packaging option mail
Reply for sample request mail
Reply for price request mail
Reply for payment negotiation mail
Thanks, mail for order confirmation
Advance payment requesting mail
Production status update mail
Delivery status update mail
Delivery delay mail
Production delay mail
Request sample feedback mail

Request for the balance payment
Request for new order order
Discount information mail
Follow up for inquiry

Frauds in Export business:

Export trade means the acquisition of goods from us by the public, by an individual, by the people, and by the company for a person who is not facing to face in another country. Here you are compelled to do business with unknown persons.

Fraudulent activities are increasingly perpetrated by fraudulent individuals claiming to give money after sending the goods by e-mail. Many newcomers in the export business get caught up in the craft of these cheats and lose money and peace of mind. So finding those cheats and passing them on is one of the most important things.

How to Know Fake Business Inquiries?

1. The e-mail will contain UNDISCLOSED RECIPIENTS in the e-mail for
     Business inquiries.
2. Usually, email starts with a generic greeting without specifying the name
     Of the company.
3. The unwanted links in the email are fake and they are fake.

4. without any business talks, they will send PROFORMA INVOICE and

   PAYMENT PROOF, there are some ATTACHMENTS in emails. They
   are fake.

5. Inquiries emailed to asking for too much quantity or too much value in
   the name of immediate need.

6. Emails, passports, government documents may be forged as proof of
   Who they are, they will email us describing their personal lives

7. E-mails from an unknown person promising 100% upfront payment

8. The e-mails sent by in the name of other NGOs are suspicious

9. The e-mails asking for our details and bank account details is a
   Frustrating experience

10. The email that comes with no business inquiry that fails to comply with our pricing is bogus.

So exporters should do a safe business without being fooled.

How to choose a SUPPLIER's?

If we are a MERCHANT EXPORTERS, the most important thing is to choose a SUPPLIER that produces the products, we have or that we have chosen

SUPPLIERS (a) MANUFACTURERS can be divided into 4 categories

The first type of SUPPLIERS

The quality plant would be great with all the amenities
There will be production texts with modern technology.

They have the power to take orders on a large scale
Infrastructure will be high
They are ISO certified companies

The second type of SUPPLIERS

*Exports to a few countries
*New technology facilities will be available
*They will be interested in exporting to new countries
*They are government-certified, and the factories of the second-generation. * Manufacturers are small compared to the first-class manufacturers

THIRD TYPE of SUPPLIERS

*Exports will be preferred but not pre-paid
*Domestic business experience
*They are not certified
*Have adequate infrastructure
*The cost will be spent on customer needs

THE FOUR TYPES of SUPPLIERS

*Factories are not standardized
*There will be no modern facilities
*It is impossible to take large orders
*They do not have government certificates
*No export experience
*SAMPLES will not be given.

So categorize the suppliers you have visited based on the above criterias and select the supplier for your export need is activity for budding exporters.

HOW TO GET THE BUYERS?

B2B Market places like ALIBABA, TRADE INDIA, INDIA MART WEBSITES, and other websites we can get Buyers for our products.

Keywords should be used more in the search engine like GOOGLE and BING, SEARCH ENGINE OPTIMIZATION, called SEO.

Participating in TRADE SHOWs globally and individually will give us BUYERS.

Documents required for export

The most important task is to prepare the documents for export after obtaining the importer. Documents required for export can be divided into two categories, before SHIPMENT and after Shipments

Document required for SHIPMENTS

1. Proforma invoice
2. Confirmation letter
3. Sales Agreement
4. Commercial Invoice
5. Packing List
6. Certificate of Origin
7. Bill of lading
8. Insurance Papers
9. Shipping Bill Copy
We will see it in detail

1. PROFORMA INVOICE

The proforma invoice should clearly state what goods are being sold to the importer at this price.

2. CONFIRMATION LETTER

The importer will confirm his order and provide it to the exporters

3. SALES AGREEMENT

The Export Agreement SALES AGREEMENT is a key document for

export and includes all bank account details. Both the exporter and the importer must sign the contract.

4. COMMERCIAL INVOICE

This document is a complete document containing all the details of the exporter's invoice number, GST number, item cost, importer details, from which port it is exported, to which port, INCOTERMS

5. PACKING LIST

PACKING LIST contains all the details such as the quantity of the product being exported and the packing method etc.

6. ORIGIN OF CERTIFICATE

It is obtained by the CHAMBER OF COMMERCE. A total of 4 sets. Its photocopier must be handed over to the bank with proof of export

7. BILL OF LADING (BL COPY)

BILL OF LADING refers to AGENTs carrying goods from the exporter. This includes detailing the product, quantity, and quality of the shipment.
The most important export document

8. INSURANCE PAPERS

Insurance sheets are very important if SHIPMENT is done in CIF PAYMENT mode. C&F AGENT will take care of this.

9. SHIPPING BILL COPY

PORT CUSTOMS AUTHORITY By SHIPPING BILL COPY
It will be presented in three headings

EXPORTER COPY
EXCHANGE CONTROL COPY
EP COPY
This document should not be given to the importer for any reason.

How to fix the price of our products in the export business.

Coming up in the form of a new export, he first named the export company. The supplier has selected and received the goods. He has made his website so that he can get orders. He has responded to business inquiries by email. Currently negotiating the price is going to the customer.

This pricing space is very important. This is where a lot of people who are stuck finalizing the orders. So understanding pricing is essential.

You can find out the pricing methods used in the export business

PRICE = COST + PROFIT

The pricing mechanism in the export business is called **INCOTERMS** (INTERNATIONAL COMMERCIAL TERMS)

Pricing Names in Export Business

1 Ex-factory Price
2 Freight on Board (FOB) Price
3 Cost Freight Price (CFR Price)
4 Cost Insurance Freight Price (CIF Price)

1. Ex-Factory Price

Ex-factory price is the cost of producing the material at the manufacturing plant and putting it in the warehouse of the factory

Ex-factory Price = Purchase Cost + Profit Local Transport Cost + Road Insurance Cost + Warehouse Cost

2 Freight on Board Price (FOB)

The importer determines an agent in our country to obtain the item from us. We add the cost of delivering the item to the importer's agent through our agent.

FOB Price = purchase cost + profit + local transport + road insurance + warehousing Cost + local transport + road insurance + clearing house expenses + bill of landing fees + Lab reports + other certification charges + inspection charges+ Banking charges + Courier charges

All added up is called FOB PRICE.

3. Cost Freight Price (CFR Price)

CFR PRICE = FOB Price + Sea freight Charges + Terminal Handling charges FOB price includes port costs such as SEA FREIGHT and TERMINAL HANDLING

4 Cost, Insurance, Freight Prices (CIF Price)

CIF Price = CFR Price + Marine Insurance

CIF Price includes shipping insurance with CFR price

Rules on pricing

1. The price of export business is always spoken in USD

2. Even if the price is stated in Indian Rupees, it should be converted to USD

3. Measurements of materials must be the same size, for example, if the metric ton = 1000 Kg, the quantity of the material must be MT. Even if it is 980 Kg it should be calculated by MT converter

4. Since the price of the dollar is fluctuating, calculate the ADJUSTED DOLLAR VALUE to calculate the cost of the goods and avoid the loss

5. ADJUSTED DOLLAR VALUE is a calculation based on the fluctuation of the value of the Indian rupee to the value of five or ten dollars, together with the price of the US dollar.

6. the most important thing. When calculating the price, 4 digit should be accurately calculated. Because even the $ 0.01 difference can cause us a huge loss.

7. Order Quantity should be converted to kilograms. For example, in kilograms, everything in kilograms should be.

8. + Adjusted Value indicates that the Indian Rupee is appreciating against the dollar and should be added at approximately +5 $ to the current value of the dollar at Rs.75.25

Let us see an example of how to set the price

You can set the price for export to the following data.

1. Purchase cost = Rs.1869 / MT

2. Profit margin = 9.89%

3. Local transport cost = Rs.8698 / order

4. Road insurance cost = Rs.1600 / order

5. Warehouse costs = Rs.10, 898 / order

6. Local transport from house to port cost = Rs.22, 698 / order

7. Clearinghouse agent costs = Rs.31, 869 / order

8. Bill of lading fees = Rs.3890 / order

9. Lab report costs = Rs.1898 / order

10. Other certificate charges = Rs.1698 / order

11. Banking charges = Rs.6898 / order

12. Courier charges = Rs.4999 / order

13. Other charges = Rs.1989 / order

14. Inspection charges = Rs.19899 / order

15. Sea freight charges = $ 4198 / order

16. Terminal handling agent charges = $ 398 / order

17. Marine inspection charges = Rs.8690 / order

18. + adjusted $ value = Rs.64.79

19. Order quantity = 23.98 MT

20. 1 Bag Quantity = 7.98 Kgs

For a bag of data above calculate,

1 Ex-factory Price

2 Freight on Board (FOB) Price

3 Cost Freight Price (CFR Price)

4 Cost Insurance Freight Price (CIF Price)

Calculate the export sales price.

1. EX-FACTORY PRICE

Ex-factory Price = Purchase cost + Profit Local Transport Cost + Road Insurance Cost + Warehouse cost

Purchase Cost in Order = Rs. 1869 * 23.98 MT

= Rs.44, 818.62 / order

Profit in Value   = Rs.44, 818.62 * 9.89%

= Rs. 4432.56

Apply these values in the calculation

Now,

Ex- factory price   = Rs.44, 818.62+Rs.4432.56 +Rs.1600+Rs.8698

= Rs.70, 447.18 / Order

Order Quantity   = 23.98 MT

So, 1 MT Value   = Rs.70, 447.18 / 23.98

= Rs.2937.75 / MT

So, 1 Kg value   = Rs.2937.75 / 1000

= Rs.2.9377 / Kg

1 Bag Quantity   = 7.98 Kgs

So 1 Bag Value   = Rs.2.9377 * 7.98

= Rs.23.44

Convert to Dollar = Rs.23.44 / + Adj. $ Value

=Rs.23.44 / 69.75

---

1 Bag Order Value in Ex – Factory Price = 0.33 $

Exercises

As per the above procedure and apply the same and find out the Export prices for the below pricing terms

2. FREIGHT ON BOARD (FOB) PRICE

3. COST FREIGHT PRICE (CFR) PRICE

4. COST INSURANCE FREIGHT PRICE (CIF)

Payment terms in export business

1. ADVANCE PAYMENT TT PAYMENT (TT - TELEGRAPHIC TRANSFER)

2. LETTER OF CREDIT (LC)

3. DOCUMENTS AGAINST PAYMENT (DP)

4. DOCUMENTS AGAINST ACCEPTANCE (DA)

5. CASH AGAINST DOCUMENTS (CAD)

Let us now discuss in detail about Beaumont methods

1. ADVANCE TT PAYMENT

If the importer claims that Advance Payment is the name of the Advance Payment, you should avoid it if the importer receives the item in advance. This is because cash transactions should only take place through the bank.

This way your money is 100 percent safe.

2. LETTER OF CREDIT (LC COPY)

The LETTER OF CREDIT is the safest way for the importer to prepare the LC document. We must accept it only if the document is SIGHT AT LC CONFIRM. And it should not be IRREVOCABLE

Let us see how this mechanism works

We provide PROFORMA INVOICE to the importer. He applied to pay LC in his bank. Once the application is accepted, the bank will certify the LC application to our bank.

The bank and our bank of that country will initiate the LC process after both the exporter and the exporter have agreed to this procedure.

When the LC AT SIGHT is in our bank, we provide the documentation for the goods after the SHIPMENT is completed. Our bank will send information to the importer's bank that we have provided everything the importer asked for. Then the importer's bank will send the documents to him after receiving the money from him. The bank of the importer will send the money from him to our bank. Our bank will give us the money.

LC AT TERMS The importer will get the documents and tell his bank that he will give the money to the bank within 30 days.

3. DP AT SIGHT (Document against Payment)

When the export process is over, we provide the documents to the bank. Our bank will send the importer's banking documents. The bank imports the documents to the importer and returns the money to the importer after the payment is made to the bank.

4. DP AGAINST ACCEPTANCE

This is not a safe money transaction method. Whenever the importer takes the goods and says in the contract that he will pay us, he will pay the money to the bank. The importer's bank will then send money to our bank. There is no guarantee that exporters will get paid in this manner so this is not a safe procedure

EXPORT CREDIT GUARANTEE COUNCIL known as ECGC may seek their help in carrying out this procedure. BUILDING EXPORTERS INCLUDE NEWS.

OPEN ACCOUNT is also available without any of the above transactions. That way Shipman Document will be shipped to couriers for exporters. There is no guarantee that the money will be available to us (exporters). In this way, the ECGC cannot help.

No document should be sent directly to the importer.

EXCHANGE CONTROL COPY-

This document is prepared for trade between the two countries.

All the necessary documents for export should be prepared and processed by the bank

Factors affecting the process of getting orders

1 Inadequate handling of sales inquiries

2. Failure to set prices for goods

3. Lack of proper FOLLOW UPS after-sales inquiry

4. Determine the highest price compared to the competitors.

5. The samples we send fail to meet BUYERS 'expectations

6. Failure to get the correct order Quantity.

7. Taking too long time to ship goods

8. When a suitable supplier is not available

How to convince the buyers to finalize the order..?

In any business negotiation, the seller and the buyer will seek to maximize their profits, so a negotiated agreement must be reached. Let's see how to canvass the importer who buys our products

1. Exporter should insist about the quality of the goods which are exported.

2. Explain about the value added services to be given apart from sending

the goods.

3. We need to realize that our product is of high quality in the market

4. Recognize the quality of packing of the goods

5. Combine some free products with products that make the customer happy.

How to send SAMPLES to Importer?

1. The importer must send samples to ensure the quality of the goods requested. That would be helpful to get the order.

2. The importer must outline the production methods.

3. After sending the samples the importer should ask for feedback on the samples.

4. Sample Cover Letter with Specimen, Size, Specifications, etc.

5. A Company Name in Samples – that helps the Importers to register the company name in their mind.

6. Samples can be sent through AIRLINE COURIER

7. To avoid the money spend on sending the samples, sometimes the exporter might request the importer to send us the item with his expected quality to make.

Role of the bankers in the export business.

All transactions in the export business must take place only through banks.

A good exporter must maintain a good relationship with the banks. Minimum balances are required to be kept in their bank accounts. Enhance goodwill with the bank by paying interest on a personal loan home loan or a loan.

If the importer claims to pay the money for the stocks send, in person, it should not be accepted.

Role of the logistics in the export business.

Three types of SHIPMENT

AIR SHIPMENT

SEA SHIPMENT

INTERNATIONAL COURIERS

Our Indian nation is geared towards global exports. Surrounded by three sides of sea and one side of the land, the geographical system makes it easy for other nations to communicate by sea and land and by air and to ship goods.

AIR SHIPMENT

This time the SHIPMENT - Airport to Airport goods is sent. AIR CUSTOMS CLEARING will take place.

Items will be sent very fast.

It is not possible to send very heavy goods.

This way the BILL OF LADING is called AIRWAY BILL

SEA SHIPMENT

In this shipment, goods sent from one port to another port. The ship here is called VESSEL.

Shipment takes place in two modes: through MOTHER VESSEL and FEEDER VESSEL (i.e stocks loaded in feeder vessel and tranasfer from feeder vessel to mother vessel at another port)

CUSTOMS CLEARING will be undertaken by the CHA agent

Safe.

You can send goods at low cost

INTERNATIONAL COURIER SHIPMENT

International couriers such as FEDEX, DHL, and TNT provide international couriers

In this manner, CUSTOMS CLEARING takes place only in New Delhi.

The most valuable engineering materials are shipped in this way

DOOR TO DOOR DELIVERY takes place

Delivery will be delivered very soon, which is very expensive.

Role of the agents in the export business

Following are the type of agents working in Export Business

CLEARING HOUSE AGENTS (CHA)
FREIGHT FORWARDING AGENTS
LINERS

CLEARING HOUSE AGENTS (CHA)

Clearing house agents are licensed representatives of the Export import business. They are responsible for INVOICE, PACKING LIST, etc., who obtain and obtain documents from us.

They submit the documents to the departmental authorities and obtain permission to export.

Explain the government's concessions to exporters.

FREIGHT FORWARDERS and LINERS will work with them.

They will receives all required documents from the port and hands it over to the exporters.

FREIGHT FORWARDING AGENTS

These are bulk agents for booking containers. They do the job of assigning us the CONTAINER BOX and bargaining with SEA FREIGHT AGENTS. They have connections to all ports worldwide. They will inspect the quality of the containers that are allocated to us.

How to convince the buyer for our payment terms?

Getting Advance Payment in Export Business is Safe for All Exporters

If the importer does not agree with the Advance Payment method, then transaction can be negotiated in a 50% Advance amount and the remaining 50% to be settled on FACTORY DELIVERY.

Most business transactions are done by the importer with a 30% advance and 70% factory delivery after payment. Try to get as much advance from the importer as possible.

Try to buy in single payment mode when the transaction value is less than $ 10,000.

More than $ 10,000 value transaction in two settlements will help to reduce bank charges.

Important Note: -

BUDDING EXPORTERS coming to the Export Industry For the sake of speeding up orders and not letting go of the order, they agree to ship the goods without any advance payment to DEMAND. This is wrong. A successful exporter needs to keep in mind that at least 30% of their PAYMENT TERMS can be delivered with Advance Payment.

How to convince the buyer for our delivery terms.

Tell the importer what time you can deliver.

Stick on to that time and try to fix 5-10 days buffer with the date, when you supplier confirmed about the finished goods to deliver.

TYPES OF CONTAINERS

1. 20 FEET CONTAINERS

2. 40 FEET CONTAINERS

3. 40 FEET HC CONTAINERS

4. 20 FEET REEFER CONTAINERS

5. 40 FEET REEFER CONTAINERS

6. OPEN TOP CONTAINERS

CONTAINER LOADABILITY

LCL - Less Container Load

FCL - Full container load

CONTAINERS MEASUREMENTS

20 Feet = 602 Cm Length, 235 Cm Width, 259 Cm Height

40 Feet = 1203 Cm Length, 235 Cm Width, 239 Cm Height

40 Feet HC Container = 1209.6 Cm Length, 234 Cm Width, 268 Cm

Height

Calculating Container Load ability

A = Volume of container

X = Volume of Carton

Volume of Carton X = Length * Breath in Cm

Total number of Carton in a container = A / X

IMPORTANT PARAMETERS IN EXPORT

Goods Packing

Goods Inspection

Goods Handling

Goods Warehousing

Goods Shifting Plan

Loading Perfection

Packing of goods

It depends on the manufacturer. It is very important to ensure in advance how the material is packed

Goods Inspection

The exporter has to go to the manufacturer's factory and ensure that the product is manufactured to the quality and quantity we expect

Goods Handling

When the material is loaded into the vehicle it is advisable to look closely at the loading point.

Goods Shifting Plan

Ensure the finished material is stacked properly in the vehicle and the container.

Loading Perfection

Ensure that the vehicle is loaded in the correct size at the right place and without any damage.

Risk Management in Export business

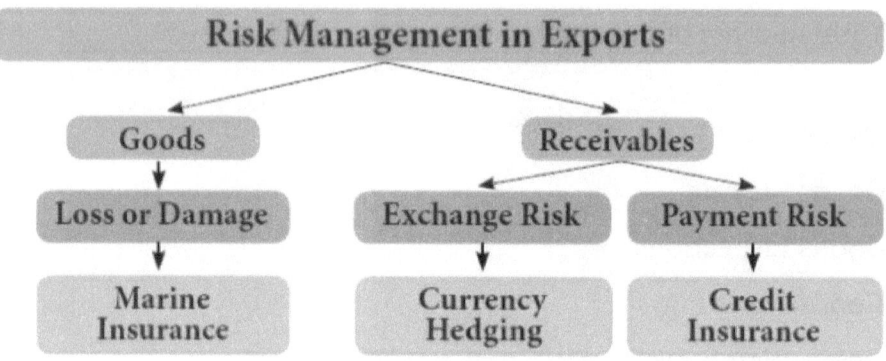

Risk in export business can be classified into three categories

1. Risk of not getting material money

2. Traffic and Marine Hazards

3. Risk of fluctuation of monetary value

The risk of non-receipt of payment for exported goods is minimized with the proper payment terms and advances received and register with insurance.

Transportation and Marine risks are minimized by insurance

Risk of fluctuation in the dollar value will be avoided by proper pricing calculation using dollar adjusted value.

EXPORT CREDIT GUARANTEE COUNCIL (ECGC)

You focus on exports. We cover the risks.

The ECGC, known as the Export Credit Guarantee Board, is run by the Government of India to help to the exporter to give the details about the countries and products to export and about the importer and their credibility.

They rank the importer by their import details. Exporters provide information on importer based on quality, which helps them to get the money from importers

Perhaps the importer offers advice on how to refund any item if the money is not paid.

Government and government subsidies, Government agencies in Export business

Government and non-governmental organizations have been doing a lot of cooperation, guidance and various promotions for exporters to increase exports

AUTHORITY
EXPORT PROMOTION COUNCIL
BOARD

AUTHORITY

APEDA - All agricultural products are included in this field. Exporters should be a member of this organization if they choose any agricultural products.

MPEDA - which includes seafood such as crab, fish etc and exporter must be a member of this organization to export products of sea foods.

EXPORT PROMOTION COUNCIL

There are a total of 28 in the Export Promotion Council.

For example,

Leather Export Council for the export of leather goods

Apparel Export Promotion Council for the export of textile

products.

Regardless of which item you choose to export, you must register as a member of the Export Promotion Council

BOARDS

There are seven boards in total
SPICES
Coffee (COFFEE)
Rubber
Tea Products (TEA)
Tobacco products (TOBACCO)
Coconut fiber products (COIR products)
COCONUT

The work of these 37 organizations is to increase Indian exports, encourage, guide and advise Indian exporters.

Service Departments for Export of India

Apart from these, some organizations offer appropriate suggestions for improving the export of that product. For example,

FOREIGN TRADE OF INDIAN INSTITUTE
INDIAN EXPORT ORGANIZATION OF FEDERATION
INDIAN TRADE PROMOTION ORGANIZATION
TRADE INFORMATION FOR NATIONAL CENTER
EXPORT CREDIT GUARANTEE CORPORATION LIMITED
EXIM BANK
PACKAGING OF INDIAN INSTITUTE

Before starting an Export firm, be prepared with the following samples

LETTER FOR LOCAL POST OFFICE

LETTER FOR BANKERS

LETTER FOR INDIAN CUSTOMS

PRODUCT SHEET WITH HS CODE REFERENCE

LAB REPORTS

MATERIAL SAFETY DATA SHEET

LETTER FOR PRODUCT SAMPLES

Important instruments required for export business

E-MAIL KNOWLEDGE

MS OFFICE WORKING KNOWLEDGE

TRACKING SHEET FOR BUYERS WHO RECEIVED SAMPLES

OFFICIAL QUOTATION SHEETS

LOCAL CLASSIFIED ADVERTISEMENT

SAMPLE SUPPLIER AGREEMENT

SAMPLE BUYER TRADER CONTRACT

Some Important Websites That Help Export Industry

www.dgft.co.in

You can apply for the IE Code through this site, Director General of Foreign Trade.

www.xe.com

www.fbil.org.in

Pricing is easy through this website

www.ginifab.com/feeds/cbm

This website helps to perform container loadability calculation

www.commerce.gov.in

All data for exporting countries exported goods and quantities for what value are available on the Government of India website

www.zauba.com

This site contains information about the exporter and importer and HSCode

www.seair.co.in

This site provides the old information needed for the export business so that we can get to know the current business environment.

Are you ready for doing export business?

We learned,

What is the export industry?
How to choose products for export
How do suppliers choose?
How to advertise our company?
We have come to know more details about the export industry with important details such as
Start an export company. Register a company first Get a PAN (Permanent Account Number) and start a bank current account.

Then apply for the IE Code through the DGFT Office. You can apply it at www.dgft.gov.in

Register in "Registration cum Membership" - RCMC Certificate to Export. Register the Promotion Council for the item you are exporting

Then start the following steps for the export business.

1. Decide on which country you are going to export

2. Select the manufacturer. If we are the manufacturer we have to find the importer.

3. Exporter must ensure delivery and payments terms by mail business inquiries

4. The Exporter should be clear about payment methods and seek to obtain advance payment and LC.

5. The Exporter must obtain the goods from the manufacturer of the required quality.

7. After receiving the goods, the relevant certificates should be produced in the documents

8. He looks for other arrangements rather than handing them over to the clearinghouse agent

9. Packing the goods and sending them to the port

10. The ship will be loaded from the port. The importer will reach the port of the country

11. Upon receipt of the payment, the importers will be handed over with the documents and he will take the stocks from the port.

12. Copies of documents should be taken. The original document will be handed over to the bank.

13. Copying and maintaining the Documents in the Office is essential

14. The GST tax account should be filed with the government through those documents

Few words for Export Entrepreneurs

Obstacles will not be visible to us until the quest for victory is within us.

The paths are wide in front of our eyes. All we have to do is walk!

No matter how hard you are in any endeavor, you can succeed in life!

So if the guys are accompanied by effort and training, success is sure... !!

Implement the tutorials and explanations provided in this book for export entrepreneurs...!!

"Congratulations on growing into a successful
export entrepreneur ...!"